W9-AUC-050

ELEVATE THE EVERYDAY

75 SIMPLE RECIPES

Editors and Content: Meghan Reilly, Kenzie Swanhart, Elizabeth Skladany, and Daniel Davis

Recipe Development: Judy Cannon, Amy Golino, Corey Mota, Robyn DeLuca, and Great Flavors Recipe Development Team

Design and Layout: Talia Mangeym and Victor Flavius

Copywriter: Karen Bedard

Creative Director: Lauren Wiernasz

Photo Direction: Lauren Wiernasz and Talia Mangeym

Photography: Michael Piazza and Quentin Bacon

Published in the United States of America by
SharkNinja Operating LLC
180 Wells Avenue
Newton, MA 02459

NN101, NN102 ISBN: 978-1-5323-0901-4

10   9   8   7   6   5   4   3   2

Printed in China.

MAKE EVERY DAY A NU DAY

Fork over the flavor and sip to your heart's content with help from the Nutri Ninja® Nutri Bowl™ DUO™. With one base and two interchangeable vessels, it easily switches from powerful Nutrient & Vitamin Extractor* to a versatile Nutrient Fusion** Processor, turning go-to ingredients into inspired drinks, snacks, and meals at the touch of a button. Together, Nutrient Fusion** and Nutrient & Vitamin Extraction* elevate your whole day. And we've got the delicious recipes and super-smart ingredient swaps to prove it.

*Extract a drink containing vitamins and nutrients from fruits and vegetables.
**Create a fusion of foods containing nutrients from fruits, vegetables, and other foods.

TABLE OF CONTENTS

AUTO-iQ BOOST™

NUTRIENT EXTRACTION*

NUTRIENT FUSION**

TIPS FOR YOUR NUTRI NINJA® CUP

TIPS FOR YOUR NUTRI BOWL™

*Extract a drink containing vitamins and nutrients from fruits and vegetables.

**Create a fusion of foods containing nutrients from fruits, vegetables, and other foods.

24

EGG MUFFINS

78

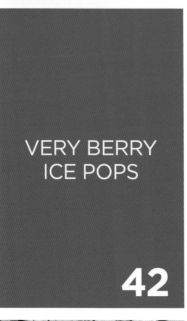

VERY BERRY ICE POPS

42

77

108

BLUEBERRY LEMON SORBET

90

CRUISE CONTROL, FOR THE KITCHEN.

Ninja® has set a new standard in drink and meal customization. Auto-iQ Boost™ gives you the power to control the texture and consistency of everything from nutritious juices and smoothies to delectable dips and doughs, all at the touch of a button.

SMOOTHIE

Using frozen fruit? Select **BOOST YES** for the smoothest results. If you're sticking to fresh fruit, you're all set with **BOOST NO**.

TO BOOST OR NOT TO BOOST?

Selecting BOOST YES or BOOST NO adds just the right amount of pulses and pauses to get the results you want from each recipe. Use this guide to get the most out of each program on your Nutri Ninja® Nutri Bowl™ DUO™.

EXTRACT

Select **BOOST YES** if your recipe includes fibrous ingredients with skins and seeds. Otherwise, use **BOOST NO**.

FUSION MIX

Nutri Bowl creations are a varied bunch. Choose **BOOST YES** for a smooth consistency; choose **BOOST NO** for a chunkier texture.

FUSION CHOP

Looking for a finer chop of fruits and veggies? Choose **BOOST YES**. Otherwise, choose **BOOST NO**.

FUSION DOUGH

Making dough for pizza or bread? Choose **BOOST YES**. For recipes with extra steps, like pie or cookie dough, choose **BOOST NO**.

NUTRIENT & VITAMIN EXTRACTION*

With the Pro Extractor Blades® Assembly and Auto-iQ™, the 1200-watt motor fully breaks down whole foods, ice, and seeds, unlocking the full potential of your fruits and veggies.†

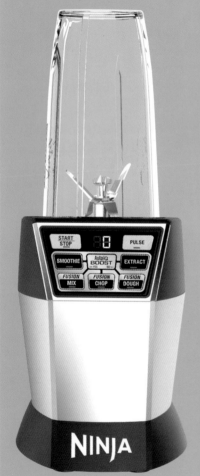

*Extract a drink containing vitamins and nutrients from fruits and vegetables.

†By blending whole fruits and vegetables, including parts that are usually discarded.

WAKE-UP EXTRACTIONS

Morning Berry
(page 18)

POWER EXTRACTIONS

Tangerine Protein Machine
(page 41)

CONCENTRATED EXTRACTIONS

Maca Coco Shot
(page 25)

SAVORY EXTRACTIONS

Jamaican Jerk Marinade
(page 33)

FROZEN EXTRACTIONS

Honey Lemon Ginger Cubes
(page 48)

SWEET EXTRACTIONS

Mocha Ninjaccino™
(page 57)

NUTRIENT FUSION*

With a 1200-watt motor, Precision Prep Blades, and Auto-iQ™, the Nutri Bowl™ pulls fresh, wholesome ingredients together to make meals vibrant with flavor and nutrients so you can savor every mouthful.

*Create a fusion of foods containing nutrients from fruits, vegetables, and other foods.

SALAD FUSIONS
Recommended program: Fusion CHOP

BLT Salad
(page 64)

FROZEN FUSIONS
Recommended program: Fusion MIX

Mango Coconut Smoothie Bowl
(page 92)

SNACK FUSIONS
Recommended program: Fusion MIX

Almond Chia Bites
(page 100)

VEGGIE FUSIONS
Recommended program: Fusion CHOP

Broccoli Tots
(page 72)

PROTEIN FUSIONS
Recommended program: Fusion CHOP

Taco Night
(page 86)

WHOLE GRAIN FUSIONS
Recommended program: Fusion DOUGH

Pear Rosemary Flatbread
(page 108)

SWEET FUSIONS
Recommended program: Fusion DOUGH

Chocolate Chip Cookies
(page 120)

TIPS FOR YOUR NUTRI NINJA® CUP

LOADING TIPS

Don't overfill the Nutri Ninja cup.
If you feel resistance when attaching the
Pro Extractor Blades® Assembly to the cup,
remove some ingredients.

5 — Top off with ice or frozen ingredients.

4 — Next add any dry or sticky ingredients like seeds, powders, and nut butters.

3 — Pour in liquid or yogurt next. For thinner results or a juice-like drink, add more liquid as desired.

2 — Next add leafy greens and herbs.

1 — Start by adding fresh fruits and vegetables.

When loading the Nutri Ninja cup, make sure ingredients do not go past the max fill line.

PREP TIPS

For best results, cut ingredients in 1-inch chunks. Do not place frozen ingredients first in the Nutri Ninja cups.

CAUTION: Remove the Pro Extractor Blades Assembly from the Nutri Ninja cup upon completion of blending. Do not store ingredients before or after blending in the cup with the blade assembly attached. Some foods may contain active ingredients or release gases that will expand if left in a sealed container, resulting in excessive pressure buildup that can pose a risk of injury. For ingredient storage, only use Spout Lid to cover.

TIPS FOR YOUR NUTRI BOWL™

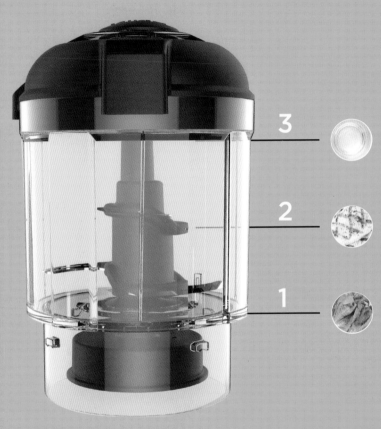

When loading the Nutri Bowl, make sure ingredients do not go past the max fill line.

LOADING TIPS

Don't overfill the Nutri Bowl or ingredients may not break down evenly. If the ingredients exceed the max fill line, take some out.

3 Add liquid on top, as the last ingredient.

2 Place heavier ingredients, like chicken and root vegetables, on top of the greens and lettuces for best results.

1 Place herbs, lettuces, and greens in the Nutri Bowl first so they are at the bottom.

PREP TIPS

Cut all ingredients to 1 1/4 inches or as designated in each recipe.

Peel bell peppers with a vegetable peeler prior to cutting for best performance.

For chopped salads with a lot of lettuce, chop the toppings separately and then layer them on top of a bed of lettuce.

EXTRACTION

CUCUMBER QUENCH

PREP: 5 MINUTES
CONTAINER: 24-OUNCE TRITAN™ NUTRI NINJA® CUP
MAKES: 1 (16-OUNCE) SERVING

MAIN INGREDIENTS

3-inch piece English cucumber, peeled, cut in 1-inch chunks

1 cup green grapes

1/2 orange, peeled, seeds removed

1/2 cup baby spinach

1/2 cup water

1/2 cup ice

CHOOSE ONE

1/3 cup honeydew melon chunks

for a fresh, sweet taste

OR

1/3 cup cantaloupe chunks

for a bold, sweeter flavor

DIRECTIONS

1 Place all ingredients into the 24-ounce Tritan Nutri Ninja Cup in the order listed.

2 Select Auto-iQ™ BOOST YES EXTRACT.

3 Remove blades from cup after blending.

RISE & SHINE

PREP: 5 MINUTES
CONTAINER: 24-OUNCE TRITAN™ NUTRI NINJA® CUP
MAKES: 1 (13-OUNCE) SERVING

MAIN INGREDIENTS

1/2 Golden Delicious
apple, peeled, cored,
cut in half

4 mint leaves

2-inch piece English
cucumber, cut in half

1 teaspoon
lemon juice

1/2 cup
green grapes

1/2 cup
coconut water

1 teaspoon
hemp hearts

1/2 cup ice

CHOOSE ONE

3/4 cup kale leaves

for a peppery kick

OR

3/4 cup spinach

for a milder flavor

DIRECTIONS

1 Place all ingredients into the 24-ounce
Tritan Nutri Ninja Cup in the order listed.

2 Select Auto-iQ™ BOOST YES EXTRACT.

3 Remove blades from cup after blending.

SPICED EYE-OPENER

PREP: 5 MINUTES
CONTAINER: 24-OUNCE TRITAN™ NUTRI NINJA® CUP
MAKES: 2 (9-OUNCE) SERVINGS

MAIN INGREDIENTS

1 ripe pear, cored,
cut in quarters

1/4-inch piece fresh
ginger, peeled

1 cup baby spinach

2 teaspoons
fresh lemon juice

Dash salt

1/2 cup frozen
mango chunks

CHOOSE ONE

1 cup brewed
chai tea, chilled

for a little spice

OR

1 cup brewed
green tea, chilled

for a fresh, green flavor

DIRECTIONS

1 Place all ingredients into the 24-ounce
Tritan Nutri Ninja Cup in the order listed.

2 Select Auto-iQ™ BOOST YES EXTRACT.

3 Remove blades from cup after blending.

DO NOT BLEND HOT INGREDIENTS.

MORNING BERRY

PREP: 5 MINUTES
CONTAINER: 24-OUNCE TRITAN™ NUTRI NINJA® CUP
MAKES: 2 (10-OUNCE) SERVINGS

INGREDIENTS

1 medium ripe banana

1 1/2 cups almond milk

3 tablespoons honey

2 tablespoons flaxseed

1 1/2 cups frozen mixed berries

DIRECTIONS

1 Place all ingredients into the 24-ounce Tritan Nutri Ninja Cup in the order listed.

2 Select Auto-iQ™ BOOST YES EXTRACT.

3 Remove blades from cup after blending.

CITRUS SPLASH

PREP: 5 MINUTES
CONTAINER: 24-OUNCE TRITAN™ NUTRI NINJA® CUP
MAKES: 2 (10-OUNCE) SERVINGS

INGREDIENTS

1 small ripe banana

1 orange, peeled, cut in half,
seeds removed

1 cup vanilla almond milk

1/2 teaspoon ground cinnamon

1 scoop vanilla protein powder

1/2 cup ice

DIRECTIONS

1 Place all ingredients into the 24-ounce
Tritan Nutri Ninja Cup in the order listed.

2 Select Auto-iQ™ BOOST NO SMOOTHIE.

3 Remove blades from cup after blending.

**SERVING
SUGGESTION**

You can top this recipe
with nuts or shredded
coconut and eat with
a spoon.

COCONUT AVOCADO TREAT

PREP: 5 MINUTES
CONTAINER: 24-OUNCE TRITAN™ NUTRI NINJA® CUP
MAKES: 4 (2-OUNCE) SERVINGS

MAIN INGREDIENTS

1 avocado,
pit removed, peeled

1 cup coconut milk

1 tablespoon agave nectar

CHOOSE ONE

1 teaspoon lime juice

for a tart, citrus flavor

OR

1 tablespoon
cacao powder

for a sweet,
chocolatey flavor

DIRECTIONS

1 Place all ingredients into the 24-ounce Tritan Nutri Ninja Cup in the order listed.

2 Select Auto-iQ™ BOOST NO SMOOTHIE.

3 Remove blades from cup after blending.

ICY ALMOND CACAO SHOT

PREP: 5 MINUTES
CONTAINER: 24-OUNCE TRITAN™ NUTRI NINJA® CUP
MAKES: 4 (2-OUNCE) SERVINGS

MAIN INGREDIENTS

1/2 cup almond milk

1 tablespoon almond butter

1 tablespoon agave nectar

1 teaspoon flaxseed

1 tablespoon cacao powder

CHOOSE ONE

2 ice cubes

for a smooth,
cool flavor

OR

1/2 frozen
ripe banana

for a creamy,
fruity flavor

DIRECTIONS

1 Place all ingredients into the 24-ounce Tritan Nutri Ninja Cup.

2 Select Auto-iQ™ BOOST YES EXTRACT.

3 Remove blades from cup after blending.

GREEN MATCHA SHOT

PREP: 2 MINUTES
CONTAINER: 24-OUNCE TRITAN™ NUTRI NINJA® CUP
MAKES: 4 (2-OUNCE) SERVINGS

INGREDIENTS

1/2 ripe banana

1/2 cup almond milk

1 teaspoon white chia seeds

1 tablespoon matcha powder

1 ice cube

DIRECTIONS

1 Place all ingredients into the 24-ounce Tritan Nutri Ninja Cup in the order listed.

2 Select Auto-iQ™ BOOST YES SMOOTHIE.

3 Remove blades from cup after blending.

MACA COCO SHOT

PREP: 2 MINUTES
CONTAINER: 24-OUNCE TRITAN™ NUTRI NINJA® CUP
MAKES: 4 (2-OUNCE) SERVINGS

INGREDIENTS

8 almonds

1 date

1/2 leaf kale, stem removed

1/2 cup coconut water

1 teaspoon maca powder

DIRECTIONS

1 Place all ingredients into the 24-ounce Tritan Nutri Ninja Cup in the order listed.

2 Select Auto-iQ™ BOOST YES EXTRACT.

3 Remove blades from cup after blending.

ACAI SHOT

PREP: 2 MINUTES
CONTAINER: 24-OUNCE TRITAN™ NUTRI NINJA® CUP
MAKES: 4 (2-OUNCE) SERVINGS

INGREDIENTS

1/2 frozen ripe banana

1 teaspoon chia seeds

2 tablespoons acai powder

1/2 cup coconut water

DIRECTIONS

1 Place all ingredients into the 24-ounce Tritan Nutri Ninja Cup in the order listed.

2 Select Auto-iQ™ BOOST YES EXTRACT.

3 Remove blades from cup after blending.

CLASSIC PEA SOUP

PREP: 5 MINUTES | **COOK:** 10 MINUTES
CONTAINER: 24-OUNCE TRITAN™ NUTRI NINJA® CUP
MAKES: 2 (8-OUNCE) SERVINGS

MAIN INGREDIENTS

1 cup frozen
peas, thawed

1 1/2 cups low-sodium
vegetable broth

1/4 medium onion

1 stalk celery, cut
in 1-inch pieces

1/2 medium
carrot, peeled, cut
in 1-inch pieces

1/2 teaspoon salt

1/4 teaspoon ground
black pepper

CHOOSE ONE

1/4 small bulb fennel,
cut in 1-inch pieces

for a licorice flavor

OR

1/4 small bulb fennel,
cut in 1-inch pieces,
and 4 fresh mint leaves

for a light, fresh flavor

DIRECTIONS

1 Place all ingredients into the 24-ounce Tritan Nutri Ninja Cup in the order listed.

2 Select START/STOP until smooth, about 40 seconds.

3 Remove blades from cup after blending.

4 Place soup in a small saucepan and bring to boil, then reduce to a simmer. Cook until heated, about 10 minutes.

DO NOT BLEND HOT INGREDIENTS.

PREPARATION SUGGESTION

This is a delicious marinade for your favorite lamb and pork dishes. Marinate for 12 hours prior to cooking.

HERB MUSTARD MARINADE

PREP: 5 MINUTES
CONTAINER: 24-OUNCE TRITAN™ NUTRI NINJA® CUP
MAKES: 1 CUP

MAIN INGREDIENTS

2 lemons, peeled, cut in
half, seeds removed

1/2 cup olive oil

1/4 cup whole-grain
mustard

2 cloves garlic,
peeled

1 teaspoon salt

1 teaspoon ground
black pepper

CHOOSE ONE

3 tablespoons fresh
rosemary, chopped

for a peppery,
woodsy taste

OR

3 tablespoons fresh
thyme, chopped

for a minty, warm flavor

DIRECTIONS

1 Place all ingredients into the 24-ounce
Tritan Nutri Ninja Cup in the order listed.

2 Select START/STOP until smooth,
about 20 seconds.

3 Remove blades from cup after blending.

CHILLED BEET SOUP

PREP: 5 MINUTES
CONTAINER: 24-OUNCE TRITAN™ NUTRI NINJA® CUP
MAKES: 3 (6-OUNCE) SERVINGS

MAIN INGREDIENTS

1 cup roasted
beets, cooled

1 clove garlic, peeled

1 cup Greek yogurt

1/2 cup low-sodium
vegetable stock

1 teaspoon apple
cider vinegar

1/2 teaspoon
lemon juice

CHOOSE ONE

2 tablespoons fresh
dill, stems removed

for an earthy taste

OR

2 tablespoons orange zest

for a sweet, citrusy flavor

DIRECTIONS

1 Place all ingredients into the 24-ounce
Tritan Nutri Ninja Cup in the order listed.

2 Select START/STOP until smooth.

3 Remove blades from cup after blending.

DO NOT BLEND HOT INGREDIENTS.

CREAMLESS CAULIFLOWER & CHICKEN SOUP

PREP: 5 MINUTES | **COOK:** 10 MINUTES | **COOL:** 20 MINUTES
CONTAINER: 24-OUNCE TRITAN™ NUTRI NINJA® CUP
MAKES: 4 (6-OUNCE) SERVINGS

INGREDIENTS

3 cups cauliflower

3 cups low-sodium chicken broth

1 medium carrot, peeled, cut in 1-inch pieces

1/2-inch piece fresh ginger, peeled

1/2 teaspoon paprika

1/2 teaspoon salt

1/4 teaspoon ground black pepper

1 1/2 cups cooked chicken, diced, warm

DIRECTIONS

1 Place all ingredients, except the chicken, into a medium saucepan. Cook over medium-high heat until cauliflower and carrots are tender, about 10 minutes. Allow mixture to cool, about 20 minutes.

2 Place cooled mixture into the 24-ounce Tritan Nutri Ninja Cup.

3 Select START/STOP until smooth, about 30 seconds.

4 Remove blades from cup after blending.

5 Reheat soup in a saucepan. Place cooked chicken in each bowl and pour hot soup on top.

DO NOT BLEND HOT INGREDIENTS.

JAMAICAN JERK MARINADE

PREP: 5 MINUTES
CONTAINER: 24-OUNCE TRITAN™ NUTRI NINJA® CUP
MAKES: 1 1/2 CUPS

INGREDIENTS

4 cloves garlic, peeled

1-inch piece fresh ginger, peeled

2 habanero peppers, cut in half, seeds removed

3 scallions, cut in 1-inch pieces

1/2 cup orange juice

1/2 cup canola oil

1/4 cup white vinegar

2 tablespoons soy sauce

2 tablespoons light brown sugar

1 1/2 teaspoons ground allspice

1 teaspoon dried thyme

DIRECTIONS

1 Place all ingredients into the 24-ounce Tritan Nutri Ninja Cup in the order listed.

2 Select START/STOP until smooth, about 20 seconds.

3 Remove blades from cup after blending.

PREPARATION SUGGESTION

Loading the protein powder after the yogurt and juice will ensure the powder gets fully blended into your drink.

STRAWBERRY BANANA PROTEIN SHAKE

PREP: 5 MINUTES
CONTAINER: 24-OUNCE TRITAN™ NUTRI NINJA® CUP
MAKES: 2 (8-OUNCE) SERVINGS

MAIN INGREDIENTS

1 small ripe banana

1/3 cup nonfat
Greek yogurt

2 scoops
protein powder

3/4 cup frozen
strawberries

CHOOSE ONE

3/4 cup orange juice
for a tart, sweet taste

OR

3/4 cup almond milk
for a nutty flavor

DIRECTIONS

1 Place all ingredients into the 24-ounce Tritan Nutri Ninja Cup in the order listed.

2 Select Auto-iQ™ BOOST NO SMOOTHIE.

3 Remove blades from cup after blending.

SERVING SUGGESTION

Add some granola as a sweet, crunchy topping.

CHOCO NUT BUTTER PROTEIN SHAKE

PREP: 2 MINUTES
CONTAINER: 24-OUNCE TRITAN™ NUTRI NINJA® CUP
MAKES: 2 (10-OUNCE) SERVINGS

MAIN INGREDIENTS

3/4 cup kale,
stems removed

1 1/2 cups unsweetened
coconut milk

1 scoop chocolate
protein powder

1 medium frozen
ripe banana

3/4 cup ice

CHOOSE ONE

2 tablespoons
almond butter

for a rich, nutty taste

OR

2 tablespoons
peanut butter

for a sweet, peanutty flavor

DIRECTIONS

1 Place all ingredients into the 24-ounce Tritan Nutri Ninja Cup in the order listed.

2 Select Auto-iQ™ BOOST YES SMOOTHIE.

3 Remove blades from cup after blending.

MANGO PROTEIN SHAKE

PREP: 2 MINUTES
CONTAINER: 24-OUNCE TRITAN™ NUTRI NINJA® CUP
MAKES: 2 (10-OUNCE) SERVINGS

MAIN INGREDIENTS

1 1/4 cups 1% milk

2 cups frozen
mango chunks

CHOOSE ONE

2 scoops vanilla
protein powder

for a sweet, light flavor

OR

2 scoops chocolate
protein powder

for a richer flavor

DIRECTIONS

1 Place all ingredients into the 24-ounce Tritan Nutri Ninja Cup in the order listed.

2 Select Auto-iQ™ BOOST NO SMOOTHIE.

3 Remove blades from cup after blending.

CHOCOLATE PROTEIN PIZZAZZ

PREP: 5 MINUTES
CONTAINER: 24-OUNCE TRITAN™ NUTRI NINJA® CUP
MAKES: 1 (14-OUNCE) SERVING

INGREDIENTS

1 ripe banana

2/3 cup almond milk

2 1/2 tablespoons sunflower butter

2 1/2 teaspoons unsweetened cocoa powder

1 scoop chocolate protein powder

1 1/3 cups ice

DIRECTIONS

1 Place all ingredients into the 24-ounce Tritan Nutri Ninja Cup in the order listed.

2 Select Auto-iQ™ BOOST YES SMOOTHIE.

3 Remove blades from cup after blending.

TANGERINE PROTEIN MACHINE

PREP: 5 MINUTES
CONTAINER: 24-OUNCE TRITAN™ NUTRI NINJA® CUP
MAKES: 1 SERVING

INGREDIENTS

1 small ripe banana,
cut in half

1 tangerine, peeled,
cut in quarters

1/2 cup spinach

1 cup water

1 scoop vanilla
protein powder

1/2 cup ice

DIRECTIONS

1 Place all ingredients into the 24-ounce
Tritan Nutri Ninja Cup in the order listed.

2 Select Auto-iQ™ BOOST YES SMOOTHIE.

3 Remove blades from cup after blending.

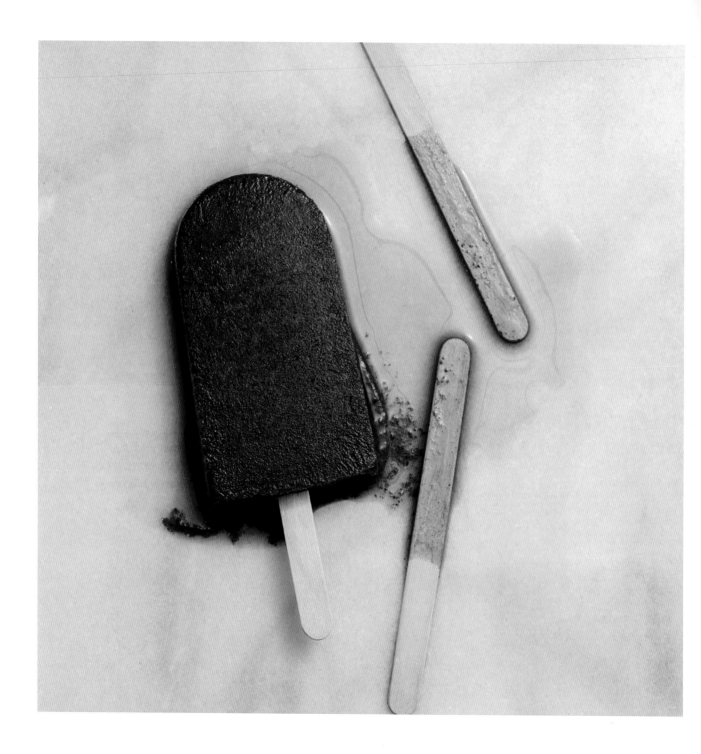

VERY BERRY ICE POPS

PREP: 5 MINUTES | **FREEZE:** 8 HOURS
CONTAINER: 24-OUNCE TRITAN™ NUTRI NINJA® CUP
MAKES: 4 (4-OUNCE) SERVINGS

MAIN INGREDIENTS

1 tablespoon lemon juice

2 tablespoons honey

1 cup frozen strawberries

1 cup frozen blueberries

CHOOSE ONE

3/4 cup
white grape juice

for a light, crisp flavor

OR

3/4 cup
pomegranate juice

for a tart flavor

DIRECTIONS

1 Place all ingredients into the 24-ounce Tritan Nutri Ninja Cup in the order listed.

2 Select Auto-iQ™ BOOST YES SMOOTHIE.

3 Remove blades from cup after blending.

4 Pour mixture into ice pop molds, and freeze for 8 hours or overnight.

WATERMELON HERB CUBES

PREP: 5 MINUTES | **FREEZE:** 8 HOURS
CONTAINER: 24-OUNCE TRITAN™ NUTRI NINJA® CUP
MAKES: 12 ICE CUBES

MAIN INGREDIENTS

3 cups watermelon, cubed

2 tablespoons sugar

Lemonade, for serving

CHOOSE ONE

12 fresh basil leaves

for an aromatic,
peppery flavor

OR

12 fresh mint leaves

for a light, fresh flavor

DIRECTIONS

1 Place watermelon and sugar into the 24-ounce Tritan Nutri Ninja Cup.

2 Select Auto-iQ™ BOOST NO SMOOTHIE.

3 Remove blades from cup after blending.

4 Pour watermelon puree into ice cube tray.

5 Rinse basil (or mint) leaves and place 1 leaf into each cube. Cover and freeze until cubes are solid, about 8 hours.

6 Serve cubes in lemonade or your favorite beverage.

INGREDIENT SUGGESTION

Try substituting
peppermint extract
for the vanilla.

FUDGY ICE POPS

PREP: 15 MINUTES | **COOK:** 10 MINUTES | **FREEZE:** 8 HOURS
CONTAINER: 24-OUNCE TRITAN™ NUTRI NINJA® CUP
MAKES: 6 (3-OUNCE) SERVINGS

MAIN INGREDIENTS

1/4 cup heavy cream

1/4 cup sugar

1 tablespoon unsweetened
cocoa powder

1 bar (3.5 ounces) dark
chocolate, chopped

1 teaspoon vanilla extract

Pinch salt

CHOOSE ONE

1 cup whole milk

for a creamy, rich flavor

OR

1 cup almond milk

for a nutty flavor

DIRECTIONS

1 Place the whole milk (or almond milk), heavy cream, sugar, and cocoa powder into a saucepan over medium heat. Cook until sugar and cocoa powder are well combined and dissolved, about 10 minutes. Let cool.

2 Placed cooled milk mixture, chocolate, vanilla, and salt into the 24-ounce Tritan Nutri Ninja Cup and let sit for 5 minutes.

3 Select START/STOP until smooth. Remove blades from cup after blending.

4 Pour mixture into ice pop molds and freeze for 8 hours or overnight.

DO NOT BLEND HOT INGREDIENTS.

HONEY LEMON GINGER CUBES

PREP: 5 MINUTES | **FREEZE:** 8 HOURS
CONTAINER: 24-OUNCE TRITAN™ NUTRI NINJA® CUP
MAKES: 18 ICE CUBES

INGREDIENTS

1 1/2 cups water

1 1/2 cups lemon juice

1/3 cup honey

2-inch piece fresh ginger, peeled, cut in quarters

1 cup raspberries

Sparkling water, for serving

DIRECTIONS

1 Place all ingredients, except raspberries and sparkling water, into the 24-ounce Tritan Nutri Ninja Cup.

2 Select Auto-iQ™ BOOST YES EXTRACT.

3 Remove blades from cup after blending.

4 Place a raspberry in each section of ice cube trays. Pour lemon ginger mixture over each berry. Freeze until cubes are solid, about 8 hours.

5 Serve cubes in sparkling water or your favorite beverage.

TROPICAL FRESH FRUIT ICE POPS

PREP: 5 MINUTES | **FREEZE:** 8 HOURS
CONTAINER: 24-OUNCE TRITAN™ NUTRI NINJA® CUP
MAKES: 4 ICE POPS

INGREDIENTS

1 cup mango chunks

2 cups pineapple chunks

2 tablespoons agave nectar

DIRECTIONS

1 Place all ingredients into the 24-ounce Tritan Nutri Ninja Cup in the order listed.

2 Select START/STOP until smooth.

3 Remove blades from cup after blending.

4 Pour mixture into ice pop molds, and freeze for 8 hours or overnight.

APPLE PIE SMOOTHIE

PREP: 5 MINUTES
CONTAINER: 24-OUNCE TRITAN™ NUTRI NINJA® CUP
MAKES: 4 (8-OUNCE) SERVINGS

MAIN INGREDIENTS

1 Golden Delicious apple, peeled, cored, cut in quarters

1 cup ice

1 cup unsweetened almond milk

1/8 teaspoon salt

3/4 teaspoon lemon juice

1/8 teaspoon ground nutmeg

1/4 teaspoon ground cinnamon

CHOOSE ONE

1 1/2 teaspoons brown sugar

for a molasses taste

OR

1 1/2 teaspoons vanilla extract

for a warm, sweet flavor

DIRECTIONS

1 Place all ingredients into the 24-ounce Tritan Nutri Ninja Cup in the order listed.

2 Select Auto-iQ™ BOOST YES SMOOTHIE.

3 Remove blades from cup after blending.

FROZEN CAMPFIRE

PREP: 5 MINUTES
CONTAINER: 24-OUNCE TRITAN™ NUTRI NINJA® CUP
MAKES: 2 (8-OUNCE) SERVINGS

MAIN INGREDIENTS

1 cup 2% milk

3/4 cup graham
cracker crumbs

1 1/2 cups chocolate
frozen yogurt

CHOOSE ONE

1/2 cup marshmallow cream

for a sweet, vanilla flavor

OR

2 tablespoons peanut butter and
1/2 cup marshmallow cream

for a nutty flavor

DIRECTIONS

1 Place all ingredients into the 24-ounce
Tritan Nutri Ninja Cup in the order listed.

2 Select Auto-iQ™ BOOST NO SMOOTHIE.

3 Remove blades from cup after blending.

PECAN PRALINE NINJACCINO™

PREP: 5 MINUTES
CONTAINER: 24-OUNCE TRITAN™ NUTRI NINJA® CUP
MAKES: 2 (10-OUNCE) SERVINGS

MAIN INGREDIENTS

1/2 cup plus 1 tablespoon
double-strength brewed
coffee, chilled

1/4 cup toasted pecans

1/4 cup 1% milk

2 tablespoons packed
dark brown sugar

1/4 teaspoon
vanilla extract

2 cups ice

CHOOSE ONE

2 tablespoons
butterscotch sauce

for a buttery, rich flavor

OR

2 tablespoons
caramel sauce

for a sweet, creamy flavor

DIRECTIONS

1 Place all ingredients into the 24-ounce
Tritan Nutri Ninja Cup in the order listed.

2 Select Auto-iQ™ BOOST YES SMOOTHIE.

3 Remove blades from cup after blending.

DO NOT BLEND HOT INGREDIENTS.

CRUSHED PEPPERMINT FROZEN FRAPPE

PREP: 5 MINUTES
CONTAINER: 24-OUNCE TRITAN™ NUTRI NINJA® CUP
MAKES: 2 (10-OUNCE) SERVINGS

INGREDIENTS

1/2 cup almond milk

2 cups low-fat vanilla frozen yogurt

10 peppermint candies

Peppermint sticks, for garnish

DIRECTIONS

1 Place all ingredients into the 24-ounce Tritan Nutri Ninja Cup in the order listed.

2 Select Auto-iQ™ BOOST YES SMOOTHIE.

3 Remove blades from cup after blending.

4 Serve in small glasses garnished with peppermint sticks.

MOCHA NINJACCINO™

PREP: 5 MINUTES
CONTAINER: 24-OUNCE TRITAN™ NUTRI NINJA® CUP
MAKES: 2 (8-OUNCE) SERVINGS

INGREDIENTS

1/2 cup plus 1 tablespoon double-strength brewed coffee, chilled

2 cups ice

1/4 cup 1% milk

1/4 cup chocolate syrup, plus more for garnish

Whipped cream, for garnish

DIRECTIONS

1 Place all ingredients, except whipped cream, into the 24-ounce Tritan Nutri Ninja Cup in the order listed.

2 Select Auto-iQ™ BOOST YES SMOOTHIE.

3 Remove blades from cup after blending.

4 Divide between 2 glasses, top with whipped cream, and drizzle with chocolate syrup.

DO NOT BLEND HOT INGREDIENTS.

FUSION

WINTER GORGONZOLA SALAD

PREP: 10 MINUTES
CONTAINER: NUTRI BOWL™
MAKES: 2 (4-OUNCE) SERVINGS

MAIN INGREDIENTS

1/4 small head radicchio, cored, cut in 1 1/4-inch pieces

1/4 small red onion, cut in 1 1/4-inch pieces

1/4 cup (2 ounces) Gorgonzola cheese

Balsamic vinaigrette, for serving

CHOOSE ONE

1/2 small apple, cut in 1 1/4-inch pieces

for a tart, sweet flavor

OR

1/2 pear, cut in 1 1/4-inch pieces, and 1/4 cup dried cranberries

for a light, sweeter flavor

DIRECTIONS

1 Place all ingredients, except dressing, into the Nutri Bowl in the order listed.

2 Select Auto-iQ™ BOOST NO FUSION CHOP.

3 Toss with balsamic vinaigrette just before serving.

CHICKEN CHOPPED SALAD

PREP: 10 MINUTES
CONTAINER: NUTRI BOWL™
MAKES: 2 SERVINGS

MAIN INGREDIENTS

1/2 cup romaine lettuce,
cut in 1 1/4-inch pieces

1/2 cup cooked
chicken breast, cooled,
cut in 1-inch pieces

1/2 cup cherry
tomatoes

Dressing, for serving

CHOOSE ONE

 +

1/4 cup feta cheese and
1/4 cup Kalamata olives

for a Mediterranean flavor

OR

1/4 cup fresh basil,
1/4 cup mozzarella cheese,
and 1 teaspoon salt

for an Italian flair

DIRECTIONS

1 Place all ingredients, except dressing,
into the Nutri Bowl in the order listed.

2 Select Auto-iQ™ BOOST NO FUSION CHOP.

3 Toss with your favorite salad dressing.

DO NOT BLEND HOT INGREDIENTS.

BLT SALAD

PREP: 5 MINUTES
CONTAINER: NUTRI BOWL™
MAKES: 2 (4-OUNCE) SERVINGS

MAIN INGREDIENTS

1/2 head Boston lettuce, cored, cut in 1 1/2-inch pieces

7 grape tomatoes (about 1/4 cup)

1-ounce chunk blue cheese, cut in half

Dressing, for serving

CHOOSE ONE

4 strips cooked bacon, cut in 1 1/2-inch pieces

for a smoky, salty flavor

OR

4 strips cooked bacon, cut in 1 1/2-inch pieces, and 1/2 avocado, peeled, cut in quarters, pit removed

for a creamier flavor

DIRECTIONS

1 Place all ingredients, except dressing, into the Nutri Bowl in the order listed. Be sure to evenly distribute ingredients.

2 Select Auto-iQ™ BOOST NO FUSION CHOP.

3 Toss salad with dressing just before serving.

GRAPE & WALNUT CHICKEN SALAD

PREP: 5 MINUTES
CONTAINER: NUTRI BOWL™
MAKES: 3 SERVINGS

INGREDIENTS

1 celery stalk, cut in quarters

1 1/2 cups cooked chicken, cooled, cubed

3 tablespoons walnuts

1/3 cup mayonnaise

1/4 teaspoon salt

1/4 teaspoon ground black pepper

1/4 teaspoon onion powder

1/4 cup red grapes

DIRECTIONS

1 Place all ingredients into the Nutri Bowl in the order listed.

2 Select Auto-iQ™ BOOST NO FUSION CHOP.

DO NOT BLEND HOT INGREDIENTS.

BRUSSELS
SPROUT SALAD

PREP: 10 MINUTES | **CHILL:** 1 HOUR
CONTAINER: NUTRI BOWL™, 24-OUNCE TRITAN™ NUTRI NINJA® CUP
MAKES: 6 SERVINGS

INGREDIENTS

1 cup Brussels sprouts,
washed, trimmed, cut in half

1 apple, cored,
cut in 1 1/4-inch pieces

Zest and juice of 1 lemon

1 tablespoon plus 1 teaspoon
unfiltered apple cider vinegar

1/4 cup extra-virgin olive oil

Salt and pepper, to taste

1/2 cup chopped
walnuts, toasted

DIRECTIONS

1 Place Brussels sprouts and apple into
the Nutri Bowl.

2 Select Auto-iQ™ BOOST YES FUSION CHOP.

3 Transfer chopped Brussels sprouts and apple to a
medium bowl.

4 Place lemon zest and juice, apple cider vinegar,
olive oil, salt, and pepper into the 24-ounce Tritan
Nutri Ninja Cup. PULSE to combine.

5 Pour dressing over salad and garnish with
toasted walnuts. Toss well. Refrigerate 1 hour
before serving.

6 Remove blades form cup after blending.

DO NOT BLEND HOT INGREDIENTS.

VEGETARIAN EGG ROLLS

PREP: 25 MINUTES | **COOK:** 20 MINUTES
CONTAINER: NUTRI BOWL™
MAKES: 6 SERVINGS

MAIN INGREDIENTS

1 3/4 cups green
cabbage, cut in
1-inch pieces

1 teaspoon
cornstarch

1 medium carrot,
peeled, cut
in 1-inch pieces

1/2 teaspoon
sesame oil

2 scallions,
ends trimmed,
cut in 1-inch pieces

1/2 teaspoon ground
black pepper

1 tablespoon
canola oil

1/4 teaspoon
ground ginger

3 tablespoons
soy sauce

6 egg roll
wrappers

CHOOSE ONE

1 stalk celery, cut in
1-inch pieces

for a fresh, green taste

OR

1 daikon radish

for a crisp, mild spice

DIRECTIONS

1 Preheat oven to 375°F. Line a baking sheet with parchment paper; set aside.

2 Place cabbage, carrot, celery (or daikon radish), and green onions into the Nutri Bowl. Select Auto-iQ™ BOOST YES FUSION CHOP.

3 Add oil to a medium sauté pan over medium-high heat. Once oil is hot, add vegetable mixture. Cook for 4 minutes, stirring occasionally, until vegetables start to wilt.

4 In a small bowl, mix soy sauce with cornstarch. Add mixture to pan with vegetables and cook for 1 minute, or until sauce thickens. Remove from heat and let cool.

5 In a small mixing bowl, combine cooled vegetables, sesame oil, pepper, and ginger. Place 2 tablespoons of mixture in center of each egg roll wrapper. Moisten edges with water. Fold 2 sides over, to look like an envelope, then roll forward to seal.

6 Coat egg rolls with cooking spray. Place on prepared baking sheet and bake 16 minutes, or until rolls are crispy and light brown, gently flipping halfway through baking.

DO NOT BLEND HOT INGREDIENTS.

INGREDIENT SUGGESTION

For a salsa verde, substitute fresh or canned tomatillos for the tomatoes.

CHIPOTLE SALSA

PREP: 5 MINUTES
CONTAINER: NUTRI BOWL™
MAKES: 4 CUPS

MAIN INGREDIENTS

1 can (14 ounces) whole
peeled tomatoes

1 white onion,
cut in quarters

1/4 cup
cilantro leaves

1 chipotle pepper
in adobo sauce

1 lime, peeled, cut in
quarters, seeds removed

Salt and pepper, to taste

CHOOSE ONE

2 tablespoons
adobo sauce

for a spicy, smoky flavor

OR

2 tablespoons
adobo sauce and
1/2 mango, peeled,
cut in quarters

for a sweet, fruity flavor

DIRECTIONS

1 Place all ingredients into the Nutri Bowl in
the order listed.

2 Select Auto-iQ™ BOOST YES FUSION CHOP.

BROCCOLI TOTS

PREP: 20 MINUTES | **COOK:** 30 MINUTES
CONTAINER: NUTRI BOWL™
MAKES: 24 TOTS

MAIN INGREDIENTS

2 1/2 cups broccoli, cut
in 1 1/4-inch florets

1/4 small onion, cut
in 1 1/4-inch pieces

1 large egg

2/3 cup panko
bread crumbs

1/4 teaspoon salt

1/4 teaspoon ground
black pepper

CHOOSE ONE

1/2 cup shredded
cheddar cheese

for a mild flavor

OR

1/2 cup shredded
pepper jack cheese

for a spicy, peppery flavor.

DIRECTIONS

1 Preheat oven to 400°F. Line a baking pan with parchment paper and coat with cooking spray; set aside.

2 In a medium saucepan, bring 1 quart water to a boil. Blanch broccoli for 1 minute. Remove broccoli and immediately plunge into ice water. Drain well.

3 Place cooled broccoli and onion into the Nutri Bowl. Select Auto-iQ™ BOOST NO FUSION CHOP.

4 Transfer mixture into a medium mixing bowl. Add egg, cheese, bread crumbs, salt, and pepper and mix thoroughly.

5 Shape mixture into 24 cylinders about 3/4 inch wide by 1 inch long. Place on prepared baking pan and bake 25 minutes, or until tots are crispy, gently flipping halfway through.

DO NOT BLEND HOT INGREDIENTS.

CAULIFLOWER RICE

PREP: 5 MINUTES | **COOK:** 6 MINUTES
CONTAINER: NUTRI BOWL™
MAKES: 2 SERVINGS

MAIN INGREDIENTS

2 cups cauliflower, cut
in 1-inch florets, divided

1 clove garlic, peeled

1 tablespoon olive oil

1 teaspoon kosher salt

CHOOSE ONE

 +

1/4 cup cilantro and
Juice of 1 lime

for a fresh, citrus flavor

OR

 +

Pinch ground chipotle
chile pepper and
1/4 teaspoon ground cumin

for a spicy, earthy flavor

DIRECTIONS

1 Place 1 cup cauliflower, cilantro (or chipotle chile pepper and cumin), and garlic into the Nutri Bowl. Add remaining cauliflower.

2 Select Auto-iQ™ BOOST NO FUSION CHOP.

3 Add olive oil to a medium sauté pan over medium-high heat. Allow oil to heat for 1 minute, then add cauliflower mixture and salt. Cook 5 minutes, or until cauliflower is tender, stirring occasionally.

4 Add lime juice (if using). Mix well before serving.

VEGGIE BURGERS

PREP: 15 MINUTES | **COOK:** 15 MINUTES
CONTAINER: NUTRI BOWL™
MAKES: 4 (6-OUNCE) BURGERS

INGREDIENTS

1/4 medium onion

1/2 medium carrot, peeled, cut in 1-inch pieces

1 can (15 ounces) white beans, rinsed, drained, divided

1/2 cup cooked quinoa

1 large egg

1/2 cup bread crumbs

1 teaspoon salt

1 teaspoon ground black pepper

1 tablespoon ground oregano

1/2 teaspoon smoked paprika

1 tablespoon canola oil

DIRECTIONS

1 Place onion and carrot into the Nutri Bowl. Select Auto-iQ™ BOOST NO FUSION CHOP. Add 1/2 the white beans to Nutri Bowl. Select Auto-iQ BOOST YES FUSION CHOP.

2 Transfer onion mixture to a medium mixing bowl. Add remaining white beans, quinoa, egg, bread crumbs, salt, pepper, oregano, and paprika. Stir to combine.

3 Divide mixture evenly and shape into 4 patties. Add canola oil to a large sauté pan over medium-high heat. When oil is hot, add patties. Cook 8 minutes, or until heated through, flipping halfway through cooking.

4 Serve over a salad or on toasted buns.

AVOCADO TOAST

PREP: 8 MINUTES | **COOK:** 5 MINUTES
CONTAINER: NUTRI BOWL™
MAKES: 4 SERVINGS

INGREDIENTS

1 ripe avocado, pit removed, peeled

1 tablespoon Sriracha sauce

4 slices Whole wheat bread, toasted

4 slices cooked turkey bacon, chopped

DIRECTIONS

1 Place avocado and Sriracha into the Nutri Bowl.

2 Select Auto-iQ™ BOOST NO FUSION CHOP.

3 Top each slice of toasted bread with pureed avocado and chopped turkey bacon.

EGG MUFFINS

PREP: 10 MINUTES | **COOK:** 23–25 MINUTES
CONTAINER: NUTRI BOWL™
MAKES: 12 EGG MUFFINS (6 SERVINGS)

MAIN INGREDIENTS

1/4 small onion

5 cherry tomatoes

7 large eggs

1/2 cup milk

3/4 teaspoon salt

3/4 teaspoon ground
black pepper

CHOOSE ONE

 +

3/4 cup baby spinach
and 1/2 cup feta cheese

for a Mediterranean flavor

OR

 +

3/4 cup green peppers
and 1/2 cup chopped ham

for a western flair

DIRECTIONS

1 Preheat oven to 350°F. Lightly coat a 12-cup
nonstick muffin pan with cooking spray.

2 Place spinach (or green peppers), feta (or ham),
onion, and tomatoes into the Nutri Bowl. Select
Auto-iQ™ BOOST YES FUSION CHOP.

3 In a medium mixing bowl, whisk the chopped mixture
with eggs, milk, salt, and pepper.

4 Divide mixture evenly between muffin cups. Bake until
knife inserted in center comes out clean,
about 23 to 25 minutes.

**SERVING
SUGGESTION**
Serve these burgers
with a spicy mayo
sauce. You can also
swap out salmon for
tuna if you prefer.

SALMON BURGERS

PREP: 10 MINUTES | **COOK:** 6 MINUTES
CONTAINER: NUTRI BOWL™
MAKES: 4 SERVINGS

MAIN INGREDIENTS

2 scallions,
ends trimmed,
cut in 2-inch pieces

1 pound uncooked
boneless, skinless
salmon, cut in
2-inch chunks

1 tablespoon
lemon juice

1 large egg

1/4 cup panko
bread crumbs

1 tablespoon salt

1/2 teaspoon ground
black pepper

CHOOSE ONE

 +

3/4 teaspoon crab
seasoning and
2 teaspoons
Dijon mustard

for a classic French taste

OR

 +

2 teaspoons soy sauce
and 3/4 teaspoon
ground ginger

for an Asian flair

DIRECTIONS

1 Place all ingredients into the Nutri Bowl in the order listed.

2 Select Auto-iQ™ BOOST YES FUSION CHOP, then PULSE 3 times. Form mixture into 4 burgers.

3 Spray a nonstick skillet or grill pan with vegetable cooking spray and place over medium-high heat. Add burgers and cook until golden brown and cooked through, about 3 minutes per side.

4 Serve on beds of lettuce or on Whole wheat buns with lettuce and tomato.

CHICKEN APPLE SAUSAGE

PREP: 15 MINUTES | **COOK:** 10–12 MINUTES
CONTAINER: NUTRI BOWL™
MAKES: 8 SAUSAGE PATTIES (4 SERVINGS)

MAIN INGREDIENTS

1/2 small onion,
cut in quarters

1 apple, peeled,
cored, cut in quarters

1 tablespoon olive oil

1/2 pound boneless,
skinless chicken thighs,
cut in 2-inch cubes

1/4 teaspoon
ground cinnamon

1 teaspoon
kosher salt

1/4 teaspoon ground
black pepper

CHOOSE ONE

6 fresh sage leaves

for an earthy, floral flavor

OR

1 teaspoon fennel seed

for a licorice flavor

DIRECTIONS

1 Preheat oven to 350°F. Line a cookie sheet with parchment paper; set aside.

2 Place the onion, apple, and sage (or fennel seed) into the Nutri Bowl.

3 Select Auto-iQ™ BOOST YES FUSION CHOP.

4 Heat the olive oil in a medium skillet over medium heat. Add apple mixture and cook, sautéing until aromatic and tender. Remove from heat and place in a large bowl to cool.

5 Place cubed chicken into the Nutri Bowl and select Auto-iQ BOOST YES FUSION CHOP.

6 Add the ground chicken to the bowl with the apple mixture. Add the cinnamon, salt, and pepper. Mix well, using your hands.

7 Form mixture into 8 patties and place on prepared cookie sheet. Bake 10 to 12 minutes, or until cooked through.

TACO NIGHT

PREP: 15 MINUTES | **COOK:** 6–8 MINUTES
CONTAINER: NUTRI BOWL™
MAKES: 8 SERVINGS

INGREDIENTS

1/2 medium yellow onion, cut in 1 1/4-inch pieces

1 pound uncooked boneless turkey breast, cut in 2-inch cubes

1 tablespoon canola oil

2 tablespoons chili powder

2 teaspoons cumin

8 hard taco shells

1 cup shredded lettuce

1/2 cup shredded low-fat cheddar cheese

1/4 cup sliced jalapeño peppers

1/3 cup cilantro

Chipotle Salsa (page 70)

DIRECTIONS

1 Place the onion and turkey into the Nutri Bowl. PULSE until finely ground.

2 Heat the oil in a medium skillet over medium heat. Sauté turkey mixture for 6 to 8 minutes, or until cooked through. Add chili powder and cumin; stir to combine.

3 Assemble each taco with cooked turkey, lettuce, cheese, jalapeño peppers, cilantro, and our Chipotle Salsa.

TUNA
TARTARE

PREP: 5 MINUTES
CONTAINER: NUTRI BOWL™
MAKES: 1 CUP

INGREDIENTS

1/4-inch piece
fresh ginger, peeled

2 tablespoons scallions,
chopped, plus more
for garnish

1 tablespoon soy sauce

1 teaspoon lime juice

1 teaspoon sesame seeds,
plus more for garnish

1 teaspoon wasabi powder

3/4 teaspoon olive oil

1/2 pound fresh sushi-grade
tuna*, cut in 1 1/4-inch chunks

DIRECTIONS

1 Place ginger into the Nutri Bowl.

2 Select Auto-iQ™ BOOST YES FUSION CHOP.

3 Add remaining ingredients to the Nutri Bowl
   in the order listed.

4 Select Auto-iQ BOOST NO FUSION CHOP.

5 Garnish with additional scallions and sesame seeds.

*Warning: This recipe contains uncooked fish.

STRAWBERRY MINT SORBET

PREP: 5 MINUTES
CONTAINER: NUTRI BOWL™
MAKES: 2 (5-OUNCE) SERVINGS

MAIN INGREDIENTS

1 1/2 cups frozen
strawberries

4 mint leaves

1 tablespoon
coconut sugar

CHOOSE ONE

1/2 cup pomegranate juice

for a tart flavor

OR

1/2 cup orange juice

for a sweet, tangy flavor

DIRECTIONS

1 Place all ingredients into the Nutri Bowl in the order listed.

2 Select Auto-iQ™ BOOST YES FUSION CHOP, then select START/STOP for 25 seconds.

SERVING SUGGESTION

For entertaining, spoon sorbet into ice cube trays and freeze. Add cubes to champagne for a festive champagne float.

BLUEBERRY LEMON SORBET

PREP: 4 MINUTES | **FREEZE:** 20 MINUTES
CONTAINER: NUTRI BOWL™
MAKES: 4 (4-OUNCE) SERVINGS

MAIN INGREDIENTS

1 3/4 cups frozen
blueberries

1 cup lemonade

CHOOSE ONE

3 mint leaves

for a light, fresh flavor

OR

1 teaspoon vanilla extract

for a warm, sweet flavor

DIRECTIONS

1 Place all ingredients into the Nutri Bowl in the order listed.

2 Select Auto-iQ™ BOOST YES FUSION MIX.

3 Place sorbet in an airtight container in the freezer for 20 minutes, or until chilled and firm.

MANGO COCONUT SMOOTHIE BOWL

PREP: 5 MINUTES
CONTAINER: NUTRI BOWL™
MAKES: 2 (8-OUNCE) SERVINGS

MAIN INGREDIENTS

1 1/2 cups frozen
mango chunks

1 tablespoon
lime juice

3/4 cup coconut milk

TOPPING IDEAS

coconut flakes

macadamia nuts

pineapple chunks

granola

blueberries

CHOOSE ONE

1/4-inch piece
fresh ginger, peeled

for a bold, sharp taste

OR

1/8 teaspoon
ground cayenne pepper

for a hotter, spicier taste

DIRECTIONS

1 Place all smoothie ingredients into the
Nutri Bowl in the order listed.

2 Select Auto-iQ™ BOOST YES FUSION MIX.

3 Transfer to bowls and add desired toppings.

BANANA SPLIT FROZEN TREAT

PREP: 4 MINUTES
CONTAINER: NUTRI BOWL™
MAKES: 3 (4-OUNCE) SERVINGS

INGREDIENTS

1/2 small frozen ripe banana, cut in quarters

1 1/4 cups frozen strawberries

1/4 cup walnut halves

1 tablespoon honey

1/2 cup light cream

Whipped cream, for garnish

Sprinkles, for garnish

Cherries, for garnish

DIRECTIONS

1 Place all ingredients into the Nutri Bowl in the order listed.

2 Select Auto-iQ™ BOOST YES FUSION MIX.

3 Serve with whipped cream, sprinkles, and cherries.

COFFEE GRANITA

PREP: 5 MINUTES | **FREEZE:** 8 HOURS
CONTAINER: NUTRI BOWL™
MAKES: 4 (3-OUNCE) SERVINGS

INGREDIENTS

2 cups strong coffee

1/2 cup sugar

2 teaspoons vanilla extract

DIRECTIONS

1 Stir together coffee and sugar until sugar dissolves. Pour coffee mixture into an ice cube tray and freeze overnight or until solid.

2 Place 7 coffee ice cubes into the Nutri Bowl.

3 Select Auto-iQ™ BOOST NO FUSION MIX.

TROPICAL FROZEN TREAT

PREP: 2 MINUTES
CONTAINER: NUTRI BOWL™
MAKES: 2 (6-OUNCE) SERVINGS

INGREDIENTS

3/4 cup frozen pineapple chunks

3/4 cup frozen mango chunks

1 tablespoon lime juice

3/4 cup macadamia milk

DIRECTIONS

1 Place all ingredients into the Nutri Bowl in the order listed.

2 Select Auto-iQ™ BOOST YES FUSION MIX.

CARROT CAKE BITES

PREP: 15 MINUTES | **CHILL:** 1 HOUR
CONTAINER: NUTRI BOWL™
MAKES: 18 BITES

MAIN INGREDIENTS

3 Medjool dates

1/8 teaspoon
ground cardamom

1/4 cup unsweetened
applesauce

1/8 teaspoon
ground ginger

1 teaspoon
vanilla extract

1 cup
shredded carrots

1 cup rolled oats

Unsweetened shredded
coconut, for garnish

1/4 cup
coconut flour

1/8 teaspoon
ground nutmeg

1/4 teaspoon
ground cinnamon

CHOOSE ONE

4 dried apricots

for a tart,
sweet flavor

OR

2 tablespoons
golden raisins

for a more
mild sweetness

DIRECTIONS

1 Place all ingredients, except shredded coconut, into the Nutri Bowl in the order listed.

2 Select Auto-iQ™ BOOST YES FUSION MIX.

3 Roll dough into 18 evenly sized bites, about 1 inch round. Roll each bite in shredded coconut.

4 Refrigerate for 1 hour before serving.

COCONUT LIME BARS

PREP: 10 MINUTES | **CHILL:** 2 HOURS
CONTAINER: NUTRI BOWL™
MAKES: 16 SERVINGS

MAIN INGREDIENTS

1 cup dried
apricots

2 tablespoons
water

1/4 cup
pumpkin seeds

1/8 teaspoon salt

2 tablespoons
hemp seed

1/2 cup unsweetened
shredded coconut

1 teaspoon
lime zest

1 tablespoon
agave nectar

CHOOSE ONE

1 cup toasted
whole macadamia

for a creamy,
mellow taste

OR

1 cup toasted, shelled
whole pistachios

for a rich, sweet flavor

DIRECTIONS

1 Line an 8 x 8-inch baking dish with plastic wrap;
set aside.

2 Place all ingredients into the Nutri Bowl in
the order listed.

3 Select Auto-iQ™ BOOST YES FUSION MIX.

4 Firmly press mixture evenly into the prepared
baking dish. Chill for at least 2 hours before cutting
into 16 pieces. Store in the refrigerator, covered, up
to 1 week.

DO NOT BLEND HOT INGREDIENTS.

SERVING SUGGESTION

These are a great snack to take with you when you are on the go to keep you feeling full and satisfied.

ALMOND CHIA BITES

PREP: 15 MINUTES | **CHILL:** 1 HOUR
CONTAINER: NUTRI BOWL™
MAKES: 24 BITES

MAIN INGREDIENTS

1/2 cup almonds

1/2 cup dark
chocolate chips

1 tablespoon
coconut oil, melted

1/2 cup
almond butter

1 tablespoon
chia seed

1 cup old-fashioned
rolled oats

CHOOSE ONE

6 Medjool dates, cut in
half, pits removed

for a rich, toffee flavor

OR

3 large dried figs

for a mildly sweet taste

DIRECTIONS

1 Place all ingredients into the Nutri Bowl in the order listed.

2 Select Auto-iQ™ BOOST YES FUSION MIX.

3 Roll dough into 24 evenly sized bites, about 1 1/4 inches round. Refrigerate 1 hour before serving.

HOMEMADE GRANOLA BARS

PREP: 15 MINUTES | **CHILL:** 30 MINUTES
CONTAINER: NUTRI BOWL™
MAKES: 18 (1 1/2-INCH) BARS

MAIN INGREDIENTS

2 tablespoons
coconut oil, melted

1/4 cup honey

1 cup granola

1/2 cup crispy
rice cereal

1/2 cup shelled
pistachios

1/4 cup semisweet
chocolate chips

CHOOSE ONE

1/4 cup
dried cranberries

for a more tart taste

OR

1/4 cup dried cherries

for a sweeter flavor

DIRECTIONS

1 Line an 8 x 8-inch baking dish with plastic wrap;
set aside.

2 Place all ingredients into the Nutri Bowl
in the order listed.

3 Select Auto-iQ™ BOOST NO FUSION MIX.

4 Spread mixture into prepared baking dish.

5 Cover mixture with plastic wrap and refrigerate
for 30 minutes.

6 Cut in 1 1/2-inch squares before serving.

DO NOT BLEND HOT INGREDIENTS.

SUPERFOOD BARS

PREP: 20 MINUTES | **CHILL:** 1 HOUR
CONTAINER: NUTRI BOWL™
MAKES: 12 SERVINGS

INGREDIENTS

1 cup raw almonds

8 dates, pits removed

1/4 cup dried cherries

2 tablespoons unsweetened coconut flakes

1 tablespoon hemp seed

2 teaspoons maple syrup

2 tablespoons toasted pumpkin seeds

1 tablespoon water

DIRECTIONS

1 Line an 8 x 8-inch baking dish with plastic wrap; set aside.

2 Place all ingredients, except pumpkin seeds and water, into the Nutri Bowl in the order listed.

3 Select Auto-iQ™ BOOST YES FUSION MIX. Scrape down sides of bowl as necessary.

4 Add pumpkin seeds and water to the Nutri Bowl and select Auto-iQ BOOST YES FUSION CHOP.

5 Press mixture firmly into the lined baking dish, cover, and refrigerate at least 1 hour.

6 Cut mixture into 2-inch squares before serving.

DO NOT BLEND HOT INGREDIENTS.

APPLE
NUTMEG BITES

PREP: 5 MINUTES
CONTAINER: NUTRI BOWL™
MAKES: 12 BITES

INGREDIENTS

1 1/2 cups dried apples

1/2 cup Medjool dates,
cut in half, pits removed

1/2 tablespoon agave nectar

1/2 teaspoon nutmeg

2 teaspoons ground cinnamon

1/2 cup toasted walnuts

DIRECTIONS

1 Place all ingredients into the Nutri Bowl
in the order listed.

2 Select Auto-iQ™ BOOST YES FUSION MIX.

3 Roll mixture into evenly sized bites, about
1 inch round.

DO NOT BLEND HOT INGREDIENTS.

TRIPLE-SEEDED BREADSTICKS

PREP: 5 MINUTES | **REST:** 1 1/2 HOURS | **COOK:** 15–20 MINUTES
CONTAINER: NUTRI BOWL™
MAKES: 6 STICKS

MAIN INGREDIENTS

1/2 cup
all-purpose flour

3 teaspoons sunflower
seeds, divided

1/2 cup
whole wheat flour

2 teaspoons poppy
seeds, divided

1 1/8 teaspoons
active dry yeast

3 teaspoons sesame
seeds, divided

1 1/2 teaspoons sugar

1/3 cup plus
1 tablespoon
warm water

3/4 teaspoon salt

4 tablespoons
olive oil, divided

CHOOSE ONE

3/4 teaspoon
coriander

for a floral flavor

OR

2 teaspoons fresh
rosemary, stems
removed, finely minced

for a piney flavor

DIRECTIONS

1 Position the Dough Blade Assembly in the Nutri Bowl, then add flour, yeast, sugar, salt, coriander (or rosemary), 1 1/2 teaspoons sunflower seeds, 1 teaspoon poppy seeds, 1 1/2 teaspoons sesame seeds, water, and 2 tablespoons oil.

2 Select Auto-iQ™ BOOST YES FUSION DOUGH.

3 Place dough ball into a lightly oiled bowl, cover loosely with plastic wrap and let rise in a warm place for 1 1/2 hours, or until it doubles in size.

4 Preheat oven to 375°F. Line a baking sheet with parchment paper. Set aside.

5 Divide dough into 6 equal portions and roll into 5-inch ropes, about 1/2-inch thick. Place onto prepared baking sheet and bake 15 to 20 minutes, or until golden brown.

6 Remove from oven and brush each breadstick with remaining 2 tablespoons olive oil. Sprinkle remaining seeds on top.

PEAR ROSEMARY FLATBREAD

PREP: 15 MINUTES | **RISE:** 1 HOUR | **COOK:** 10-15 MINUTES
CONTAINER: NUTRI BOWL™
MAKES: 4-6 SERVINGS

MAIN INGREDIENTS

2/3-3/4 cup warm
water (110°F-115°F)

1 1/4 cups
Whole wheat flour

1 packet
(2 1/4 teaspoons)
active dry yeast

Cornmeal,
for dusting

1 teaspoon salt

1 large pear,
thinly sliced

1 tablespoon sugar

2 tablespoons fresh
rosemary, stems
removed, minced

1/4 cup extra-virgin
olive oil

1 cup unbleached,
all-purpose flour

CHOOSE ONE

1/2 cup shredded
Gruyère cheese

for a nutty,
mellow flavor

OR

1/2 cup crumbled
Gorgonzola cheese

for a creamy,
earthy flavor

DIRECTIONS

1 Preheat oven to 450°F.

2 Position the Dough Blade Assembly in the Nutri Bowl, then add water, yeast, salt, and sugar; PULSE to combine.

3 Add oil and flours, and select Auto-iQ™ BOOST YES FUSION DOUGH until a loose ball forms. Transfer dough to a lightly oiled bowl and cover. Let rise for 1 hour.

4 Sprinkle a 10 x 15-inch baking sheet with cornmeal and roll out or press the dough into a thin round. Lay pear slices on top and sprinkle evenly with shredded cheese.

5 Bake 10 to 15 minutes, or until cheese has melted and crust is golden brown. Garnish with fresh rosemary.

WHOLE WHEAT CRACKERS

PREP: 8 MINUTES | **COOK:** 14 MINUTES
CONTAINER: NUTRI BOWL™
MAKES: 8 SERVINGS

MAIN INGREDIENTS

1/2 cup all-
purpose flour

1/2 cup
whole wheat flour

1/2 teaspoon salt

1/2 teaspoon ground
black pepper

2 tablespoons cold unsalted
butter, cut in 1/2-inch pieces

1/3 cup water

CHOOSE ONE

1 teaspoon
Italian seasoning

for a savory Italian flavor

OR

1 teaspoon fresh thyme

for a classic
French flavor

DIRECTIONS

1 Preheat oven to 400°F.

2 Place all ingredients, except water, into the Nutri Bowl. PULSE until ingredients are combined and butter forms pea-sized pieces.

3 Select Auto-iQ™ BOOST YES FUSION DOUGH and while machine is running, drizzle in the water until a dough ball forms.

4 Turn the dough out onto a large piece of plastic wrap. Press it into a 1-inch thick disk. Wrap tightly in plastic wrap and refrigerate for 1 hour.

5 Place dough onto a lightly floured surface and roll into a rectangle, about 1/8-inch thick. Place the rolled dough onto an ungreased baking sheet. Prick dough with a fork and cut in desired cracker shapes.

6 Bake 14 minutes, or until light golden brown. Let cool completely.

QUICK
FRIED RICE

PREP: 15 MINUTES
CONTAINER: NUTRI BOWL™
MAKES: 4 (4-OUNCE) SERVINGS

INGREDIENTS

1 medium carrot, peeled,
cut in 1-inch pieces

1/2 small onion, peeled,
cut in quarters

2 cloves garlic, peeled

1/4-inch piece
fresh ginger, peeled

1 package 100% brown rice
(90-second cook time)

1 tablespoon peanut oil

1/2 cup peas

1/2 teaspoon sesame oil

1 1/2 tablespoons soy sauce

2 scallions, thinly sliced

1/4 teaspoon red pepper flakes

DIRECTIONS

1 Place carrot, onion, garlic, ginger, and brown rice
into the Nutri Bowl.

2 Select Auto-iQ™ BOOST NO FUSION CHOP.

3 Heat peanut oil in a large skillet over medium high
heat. Add rice and vegetable mixture and cook for
5 minutes, stirring occasionally. Stir in peas, sesame
oil, soy sauce, scallions, and red pepper flakes.
Cook until heated through.

DO NOT BLEND HOT INGREDIENTS.

WHOLE WHEAT PIZZA DOUGH

PREP: 5 MINUTES | **REST:** 1 HOUR | **COOK:** 10–15 MINUTES
CONTAINER: NUTRI BOWL™
MAKES: 2 (10-INCH) PIZZA DOUGHS

INGREDIENTS

1 packet (2 1/4 teaspoons) active dry yeast

1 1/2 teaspoons sugar

2/3 cup warm water

1 cup all-purpose flour

1 cup whole wheat flour

1/2 teaspoon salt

1/4 cup extra-virgin olive oil

DIRECTIONS

1 Combine the yeast, sugar, and warm water in a small bowl and set aside until foamy, about 5 minutes.

2 Position the Dough Blade Assembly in the Nutri Bowl, then add the flours, salt, olive oil, and yeast mixture.

3 Select Auto-iQ™ BOOST YES FUSION DOUGH.

4 Place dough ball into a lightly oiled bowl and cover loosely with plastic wrap. Let rise in a warm place for 1 hour or until double in size.

5 Preheat oven to 450°F.

6 Cut dough ball in half. Roll out one half to desired thickness and place on a lightly oiled pan. Repeat with other half, or cover in plastic wrap and store in freezer for up to 2 months.

7 Top with your favorite pizza toppings. Bake 10 to 15 minutes.

ZUCCHINI QUICK BREAD

PREP: 15 MINUTES | **COOK:** 1 HOUR
CONTAINER: NUTRI BOWL™
MAKES: 1 LOAF (12 SERVINGS)

MAIN INGREDIENTS

1 medium zucchini
(2 cups), cut in
1-inch cubes

1 1/2 cups
all-purpose flour

1 egg plus
1 egg yolk

1/2 teaspoon salt

1 cup
granulated sugar

3/4 teaspoon
baking soda

1/2 cup
vegetable oil

1 1/2 teaspoons
ground cinnamon

2 teaspoons
vanilla extract

CHOOSE ONE

1/2 cup pecans,
coarsely chopped

for a nutty flavor

OR

1/2 cup chocolate chips

for a rich, sweet flavor

DIRECTIONS

1 Preheat oven to 375°F.
Lightly spray an 8 1/2 x 4 1/2 x 2 1/2-inch loaf pan
with nonstick cooking spray; set aside.

2 Place zucchini, egg and yolk, sugar, oil, and vanilla into
the Nutri Bowl.

3 Select Auto-iQ™ BOOST NO FUSION DOUGH. Add flour,
salt, baking soda, cinnamon, and pecans (or chocolate
chips) and select Auto-iQ BOOST NO FUSION DOUGH.

4 Pour batter into prepared pan. Bake 1 hour, or until knife
inserted in center comes out clean.

LEMON POUND CAKE

PREP: 10 MINUTES | **COOK:** 40–50 MINUTES
CONTAINER: NUTRI BOWL™
MAKES: 12 SERVINGS

MAIN INGREDIENTS

3/4 cup
granulated sugar

1/4 teaspoon
kosher salt

1 stick unsalted butter,
sliced, softened

Powdered sugar,
for dusting

2 eggs

Juice of 1/2
lemon

1 cup unbleached
all-purpose flour

1 teaspoon
baking powder

CHOOSE ONE

Zest of 1 lemon, cut in
half, seeds removed

for a slightly
more tart flavor

OR

1/2 teaspoon
dried lavender

for a more floral flavor

DIRECTIONS

1 Preheat oven to 350°F. Line a 7 3/8 x 3 5/8 x 2-inch loaf pan with parchment paper. Lightly spray with cooking oil.

2 Position the Dough Blade Assembly in the Nutri Bowl, then add sugar and butter. Select Auto-iQ™ BOOST YES FUSION DOUGH.

3 Add eggs, lemon juice, and lemon zest (or dried lavender) to the Nutri Bowl and select Auto-iQ BOOST NO FUSION DOUGH.

4 Add flour, baking powder, and salt to the Nutri Bowl and select Auto-iQ BOOST NO FUSION DOUGH.

5 Spread dough into prepared loaf pan.

6 Bake for 40 to 50 minutes, or until cake is cooked through and top is golden brown.

7 Cool cake completely and remove from pan. Dust with powdered sugar.

NO-BAKE MINI CHEESECAKES

PREP: 25 MINUTES | **CHILL:** 4 HOURS
CONTAINER: NUTRI BOWL™
MAKES: 12 SERVINGS

MAIN INGREDIENTS

1 sleeve (2 1/2 cups)
honey graham
crackers, chopped

1/4 cup
granulated sugar

1/4 cup light
brown sugar

1/2 teaspoon
vanilla extract

1/4 cup
(4 tablespoons)
unsalted
butter, melted

1 tub (8 ounces)
whipped topping,
thawed

1 package
(8 ounces) cream
cheese, softened

CHOOSE ONE

1 teaspoon lemon juice

for a tart, citrus flavor

OR

+

1 teaspoon lemon juice and
1/4 cup peanut butter

for a nutty flavor

DIRECTIONS

1 Line a standard 12-cup muffin tin with paper or aluminum liners. Lightly coat the inside of liners with cooking spray. Set pan aside.

2 Place graham crackers, brown sugar, and butter into the Nutri Bowl.

3 Select Auto-iQ™ BOOST NO FUSION MIX.

4 Divide mixture evenly in the prepared muffin tin. Press on mixture until firmly packed. Set pan aside.

5 Place cream cheese, granulated sugar, lemon juice (or lemon juice and peanut butter), and vanilla into the Nutri Bowl.

6 Select Auto-iQ BOOST NO FUSION MIX. Remove lid and scrape down sides of bowl. Select START/STOP for 15 seconds, or until mixture is creamy and well combined.

7 Spoon cream cheese mixture into a bowl and gently fold in whipped topping until evenly incorporated.

8 Spoon cheesecake mixture into prepared muffin tins and spread to level it. Refrigerate at least 4 hours or overnight before serving.

CHOCOLATE CHIP COOKIES

PREP: 10 MINUTES | **COOK:** 10–12 MINUTES
CONTAINER: NUTRI BOWL™
MAKES: 20 COOKIES

MAIN INGREDIENTS

1 egg

1/2 teaspoon
vanilla extract

1/4 cup plus
2 tablespoons
granulated sugar

1 cup plus 2
tablespoons flour

1/4 cup plus
2 tablespoons
brown sugar

1/2 teaspoon
salt

1 stick unsalted
butter, cut in
pieces, softened

1/2 teaspoon
baking soda

CHOOSE ONE

1 cup chocolate chips

for a rich, sweet flavor

OR

1 cup chocolate chips and
1/2 cup chopped walnuts

for a sweet, nutty flavor

DIRECTIONS

1 Preheat oven to 375°F.

2 Position the Dough Blade Assembly in the Nutri Bowl, then add egg, sugars, butter, and vanilla. Select Auto-iQ™ BOOST NO FUSION DOUGH.

3 Add flour, salt, and baking soda to the Nutri Bowl. Select Auto-iQ BOOST YES FUSION DOUGH until just combined.

4 Transfer dough to a large mixing bowl. Stir in chocolate chips.

5 Scoop heaping teaspoons of dough onto an ungreased baking sheet, about 2 inches apart.

6 Bake 10 to 12 minutes, or until golden brown.

SERVING SUGGESTION

Enjoy atop a bowl of fresh berries for a quick and impressive dessert.

DARK CHOCOLATE CHIP MOUSSE

PREP: 5 MINUTES
CONTAINER: NUTRI BOWL™
MAKES: 3 CUPS (4–6 SERVINGS)

INGREDIENTS

1 1/2 cups coconut cream, chilled

1/4 cup dark chocolate syrup

1/3 cup semisweet chocolate chips

DIRECTIONS

1. Place all ingredients into the Nutri Bowl in the order listed.

2. Select Auto-iQ™ BOOST NO FUSION MIX.

APPLE CIDER MUFFINS

PREP: 10 MINUTES | **COOK:** 20 MINUTES
CONTAINER: NUTRI BOWL™
MAKES: 12 MUFFINS

INGREDIENTS

1 medium apple, cored, cut in 1 1/4-inch pieces

3/4 cup apple cider

2 large eggs

2 tablespoons vegetable oil

Zest and juice of 1 medium lemon (1 tablespoon lemon juice)

1 cup Whole wheat flour

1 cup all-purpose flour

2/3 cup brown sugar, packed

1/2 cup granola

1 tablespoon baking powder

1/2 teaspoon ground cinnamon

1/2 teaspoon salt

DIRECTIONS

1 Preheat oven to 350°F. Lightly spray a standard 12-cup muffin tin with nonstick cooking spray, or use muffin liners.

2 Place apple in the Nutri Bowl. Select Auto-iQ™ BOOST YES FUSION CHOP. Transfer chopped apple to a large mixing bowl; set aside.

3 Place cider, eggs, oil, lemon zest, and lemon juice into the Nutri Bowl. Select Auto-iQ BOOST NO FUSION MIX.

4 Add remaining ingredients to the Nutri Bowl. Select Auto-iQ BOOST NO FUSION MIX.

5 Pour batter over chopped apples and stir gently to combine.

6 Pour into prepared muffin tin. Bake 20 minutes, or until golden brown and cooked through.

BONUS

SUN-DRIED
TOMATO SAUCE

PREP: 5 MINUTES | **COOK:** 20–25 MINUTES
CONTAINER: 24-OUNCE TRITAN™ NUTRI NINJA® CUP
MAKES: 2–4 SERVINGS

INGREDIENTS

1/2 onion, peeled,
cut in quarters

1/2 tablespoon canola oil

2 cloves garlic, peeled

1 can (14 ounces) whole
peeled tomatoes and juice

1 jar (3 ounces) sun-dried
tomatoes packed in olive oil

1/4 cup dry red wine

1/4 teaspoon red pepper flakes

1/4 cup fresh basil, chopped

Salt and pepper, to taste

DIRECTIONS

1 Place all ingredients into the 24-ounce
Tritan Nutri Ninja Cup in the order listed.

2 Select START/STOP until desired consistency
is reached.

3 Remove blades from cup after blending.

4 Place sauce into a medium saucepan and bring to a
boil over medium heat. Reduce heat and simmer 20
to 25 minutes.

DO NOT BLEND HOT INGREDIENTS.

EVERYDAY VINAIGRETTE

PREP: 15 MINUTES
CONTAINER: 24-OUNCE TRITAN™ NUTRI NINJA® CUP
MAKES: 1 1/4 CUPS

INGREDIENTS

1/2 cup cilantro leaves

1/3 cup fresh flat-leaf
parsley leaves

2 tablespoons chives,
roughly chopped

1 clove garlic, peeled

1/4 teaspoon salt

1/4 teaspoon ground
black pepper

1 tablespoon Dijon mustard

1/4 cup apple cider vinegar

3/4 cup extra-virgin olive oil

DIRECTIONS

1 Place all ingredients, into the 24-ounce Tritan
Nutri Ninja Cup in the order listed.

2 Select START/STOP until desired consistency
is reached.

SUPREME GODDESS DRESSING

PREP: 15 MINUTES
CONTAINER: 24-OUNCE TRITAN™ NUTRI NINJA® CUP
MAKES: 2 CUPS

INGREDIENTS

1/3 cup rice wine vinegar

3 garlic cloves, peeled

1/4 cup Dijon mustard

1/2 teaspoon kosher salt

1/4 teaspoon ground
black pepper

1/4 cup light mayonnaise

1/2 cup fresh flat-leaf
parsley leaves

1/4 cup fresh tarragon

1/4 cup fresh dill,
stems removed

2 scallions, ends trimmed,
cut in 1-inch pieces

1 cup nonfat cottage cheese

1/2 cup extra-virgin olive oil

DIRECTIONS

1 Place all ingredients into the 24-ounce
Tritan Nutri Ninja Cup in the order listed.

2 Select START/STOP and blend for 20 seconds,
or until desired consistency is reached.

3 Remove blades from cup after blending.

PESTO

PREP: 5 MINUTES
CONTAINER: NUTRI BOWL™
MAKES: 4–6 SERVINGS

INGREDIENTS

1/4 cup toasted pine nuts

2 large cloves garlic, peeled

1 1/2 cups fresh basil

1/4 cup grated
Parmesan cheese

1/4 teaspoon salt

1/4 teaspoon
ground black pepper

1/3 cup extra-virgin olive oil

DIRECTIONS

1 Place all ingredients into the Nutri Bowl in the order listed.

2 Select Auto-iQ™ BOOST YES FUSION MIX.

DO NOT BLEND HOT INGREDIENTS.

ROMESCO SAUCE

PREP: 15 MINUTES
CONTAINER: NUTRI BOWL™
MAKES: 2 CUPS

INGREDIENTS

1 red bell pepper, roasted, peeled, seeds removed

1/4 cup dry-roasted almonds

3-inch piece baguette, cut in 1-inch cubes

1 clove garlic, peeled

1 tablespoon drained capers

2 anchovy fillets

1 tablespoon sherry vinegar

Juice of 1/2 lemon

1/2 teaspoon honey

3 tablespoons olive oil

1/2 teaspoon smoked paprika

1/4 teaspoon red pepper flakes

Salt and pepper, to taste

DIRECTIONS

1 Place all ingredients, except salt and pepper, into the Nutri Bowl in the order listed.

2 Select START/STOP until desired consistency is reached.

3. Add salt and pepper to taste.

DO NOT BLEND HOT INGREDIENTS.

INDEX

BONUS

MAXIMIZE YOUR DUO™

Get the most out of your Duo with some of our most popular accessories.

   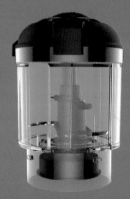

12 OZ. TRITAN™ NUTRI NINJA® CUP

Perfect for kid-size, portion-controlled drinks and to-go snacks.

18 OZ. TRITAN NUTRI NINJA CUP

Make this your go-to cup for smoothies at home or on the go.

32 OZ. TRITAN NUTRI NINJA CUP

The ideal size to create a generous drink for yourself, with plenty to share if you like.

NINJA NUTRI BOWL™ WITH DRIZZLE HOLE LID

No need to dirty another container—simply seal and store leftovers in the fridge with this innovative lid.

Shop ninjaaccessories.com for these signature Ninja® accessories and many more.

Want exclusive deals, how-to videos, recipes, and more?
Register your Ninja product at registeryourninja.com